Animals with Superpowers

PHASE 5

/u/ow/

Level 7 – Turquoise

Helpful Hints for Reading at Home

The graphemes (written letters) and phonemes (units of sound) used throughout this series are aligned with Letters and Sounds. This offers a consistent approach to learning whether reading at home or in the classroom.

HERE IS A LIST OF PHONEMES FOR THIS PHASE OF LEARNING. AN EXAMPLE OF THE PRONUNCIATION CAN BE FOUND IN BRACKETS.

Phase 5			
ay (day)	ou (out)	ie (tie)	ea (eat)
oy (boy)	ir (girl)	ue (blue)	aw (saw)
wh (when)	ph (photo)	ew (new)	oe (toe)
au (Paul)	a_e (make)	e_e (these)	i_e (like)
o_e (home)	u_e (rule, cube)		

Phase 5 Alternative Pronunciations of Graphemes			
a (hat, what)	e (bed, she)	i (fin, find)	o (hot, so, other)
u (but, unit)	c (cat, cent)	g (got, giant)	ow (cow, blow)
ie (tied, field)	ea (eat, bread)	er (farmer, herb)	ch (chin, school, chef)
y (yes, by, very)	ou (out, shoulder, could, you)		

HERE ARE SOME WORDS WHICH YOUR CHILD MAY FIND TRICKY.

Phase 5 Tricky Words			
oh	their	people	Mr
Mrs	looked	called	asked
could			

TOP TIPS FOR HELPING YOUR CHILD TO READ:

• Allow children time to break down unfamiliar words into units of sound and then encourage children to string these sounds together to create the word.

• Encourage your child to point out any focus phonics when they are used.

• Read through the book more than once to grow confidence.

• Ask simple questions about the text to assess understanding.

• Encourage children to use illustrations as prompts.

PHASE 5

/u/ow/

This book focuses on the alternative pronunciations of the graphemes /u/ and /ow/ and is a Turquoise level 7 book band.

Can you sort these words into two groups? One group has ow as in **now**. One group has ow as in **blow**.

glow

cow

town

snow

down

show

power

grown

Do you want to have a superpower? Do you want to glow in the dark? What about rapid speed? Those are both cool powers!

What power do you want?

Superpowers might not be real for humans, but some animals can do things that are just like having superpowers! Some can see in the dark and some can regrow parts of their bodies.

Some animals can see in the dark. The leaf-tailed gecko can see much better at night than humans can.

How well can you see in the dark?

Cats' pupils are a slit shape. When there is low light, cats' pupils grow wide to let in more light. This helps them to see in the dark!

Pupil

Some animals have the power to regrow their different parts. Humans can grow back nails and hair but not an arm or a leg.

When a shark's teeth come out, it is not a problem. Sharks have rows of teeth that can regrow. They can regrow around 30,000 teeth in a lifetime.

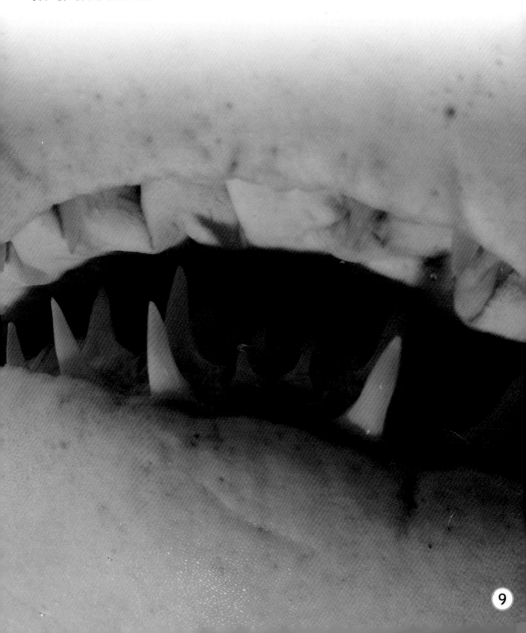

Starfish can have lots of arms. If a starfish has lost some of its arms, it can grow them back.

This starfish will grow the missing arm back.

Some animals have the power to make it seem like they have disappeared. The bottom side of the glass frog is clear. This means it can blend in with whatever it sits on.

Lots of animals use their bodies to protect them. The skunk has a clever way to do this, but it comes with an awful smell.

Skunks have a gland near their bum. They lift up their tail to an attacker, show the gland and then spray an awful smelling liquid over them!

Some animals attack other animals. Bulls have big horns. They can attack different bulls to show them how powerful they are.

If you had a superpower, what might it be? Can you draw it? You might have horns like a bull or pupils to see in low light like a cat!

©2022 **BookLife Publishing Ltd.**
King's Lynn, Norfolk PE30 4LS

ISBN 978-1-80155-108-3

All rights reserved. Printed in Poland.
A catalogue record for this book is available
from the British Library.

Animals with Superpowers
Written by William Anthony
Designed by Gareth Liddington

An Introduction to BookLife Readers...

Our Readers have been specifically created in line with the London Institute of Education's approach to book banding and are phonetically decodable and ordered to support each phase of the Letters and Sounds document.

Each book has been created to provide the best possible reading and learning experience. Our aim is to share our love of books with children, providing both emerging readers and prolific page-turners with beautiful books that are guaranteed to provoke interest and learning, regardless of ability.

BOOK BAND GRADED using the Institute of Education's approach to levelling.

PHONETICALLY DECODABLE supporting each phase of Letters and Sounds.

EXERCISES AND QUESTIONS to offer reinforcement and to ascertain comprehension.

CLEAR DESIGN to inspire and provoke engagement, providing the reader with clear visual representations of each non-fiction topic.

AUTHOR INSIGHT:
WILLIAM ANTHONY

Despite his young age, William Anthony's involvement with children's education is quite extensive. He has written over 60 titles with BookLife Publishing so far, across a wide range of subjects. William graduated from Cardiff University with a 1st Class BA (Hons) in Journalism, Media and Culture, creating an app and a TV series, among other things, during his time there.

William Anthony has also produced work for the Prince's Trust, a charity created by HRH The Prince of Wales that helps young people with their professional future. He has created animated videos for a children's education company that works closely with the charity.

PHASE 5

/u/ow/

This book focuses on the alternative pronunciations of the graphemes /u/ and /ow/ and is a Turquoise level 7 book band.

Image Credits Images are courtesy of Shutterstock.com. With thanks to Getty Images, Thinkstock Photo and iStockphoto. Cover – p4–5 – Rawpixel.com, IrinaK. p6–7 – Miguel Scmitter, Maud de Vries. p8–9 – milatas, Greg Amptman. p10–11 – 384, petrdd. p12–13 – Geoffrey Kuchera, MyImages – Micha. p14–15 – alberto clemares exposito,